What Do SPRINGS Do?

Heinemann
LIBRARY

David Glover

www.heinemann.co.uk/library
Visit our website to find out more information about Heinemann Library books.

To order:
 Phone 44 (0) 1865 888066
Send a fax to 44 (0) 1865 314091
Visit the Heinemann Bookshop at www.heinemann.co.uk/library to browse our
 catalogue and order online.

First published in Great Britain by Heinemann Library,
Halley Court, Jordan Hill, Oxford OX2 8EJ, part
of Harcourt Education. Heinemann is a registered
trademark of Harcourt Education Ltd.

Editorial: Clare Lewis and Katie Shepherd
Design: Victoria Bevan and Q2A Creative
Illustrations: Barry Atkinson (pp9, 17) and Tony
Kenyon (pp7, 13, 21)
Picture Research: Mica Brancic
Production: Helen McCreath
Printed and bound in China by WKT Company
Limited

10 digit ISBN 0 431 06404 0
13 digit ISBN 978 0 431 06404 8
10 09 08 07 06
10 9 8 7 6 5 4 3 2 1

British Library Cataloguing in Publication Data
Glover, David
What do springs do? - 2nd Edition
621.8'24
A full catalogue record for this book is available from
the British Library.

Acknowledgements
The publishers would like to thank the following for
permission to reproduce photographs: Trevor Clifford
pp1, 4, 5, 6, 9, 10, 12, 13, 15, 18, 19, 20, 21; Sealy
p8; Spectrum Colour Library p14; Stockfile/Steven
Behr p16; Zefa p17.

Cover photograph reproduced with permission of
Corbis.

The publishers would like to thank Angela Royston for
her assistance in the preparation of this book.

Every effort has been made to contact copyright
holders of any material reproduced in this book. Any
omissions will be rectified in subsequent printings if
notice is given to the publishers.

The paper used to print this book comes from
sustainable resources.

Any words appearing in the text in bold, **like this**, are
explained in the Glossary

Contents

What are springs?

Most springs are made from metal wire or strips. If you squash a spring, stretch it, bend it, or wind it up, it always tries to spring back into shape.

This jack-in-a-box is a spring toy. When you push it down into the box and fasten the lid, you are squashing its spring.

When you unfasten the **catch,** the spring makes the jack jump from its box. It can make you jump with surprise!

5

Pogo stick

A pogo stick has a strong spring that bounces you up in the air. A rubber foot stops the stick from slipping on the ground.

 **Pogo crazy**

In 1999, Ashrita Furman used a pogo stick to jump up the 1,899 steps of the CN Tower in Ontario, Canada.

The spring on a pogo stick is a strong **spiral** of steel wire. Your weight squashes it down to make it shorter. The spring pushes back up as it tries to return to its normal shape. This force lifts you up into the air.

When you jump with a pogo stick, you squash the spring.

The spring pushes back up and bounces you into the air.

When you land, the spring squashes again ready for the next bounce.

Spring beds and chairs

Have you ever bounced on your bed? Many bed mattresses are filled with wire springs. These help you to sleep comfortably at night. When you lie on the bed, the springs squash to support every part of your body.

The springs on this chair make the seat soft and comfy. When you sit on this chair the springs stretch to hold up your weight.

Spring words

compression

relaxed spring

tension

When a spring is made shorter, or squashed, we say that it is compressed. When a spring is made longer, or stretched, we say that it is in tension.

Door springs and locks

This gate has a spring at the top. It pulls the gate shut when someone leaves it open.

This door has a spring at the bottom. It stops the door from banging against the wall when someone pushes it open too hard.

The door handle has a spring inside.
When you turn the handle it pulls
back the **catch**. When you let go
of the handle the spring pushes
the catch back into place.

The door spring and the catch spring
work together to keep the door shut.

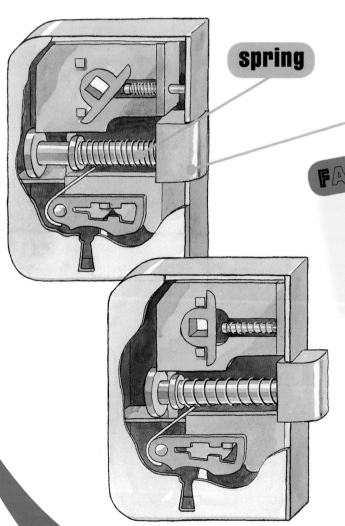

spring

catch

FACT FILE Old springs

The first known metal springs are
parts of old door locks. Some are
more than 500 years old.

Spring loaded

This pen has a spring inside it. We say that the pen is **spring loaded**. When you press the button at the bottom, the pen tip comes out of the case. A spring tries to push the tip back inside, but a **catch** holds it in place. When you press the button again, this releases the catch and the tip goes back inside the pen case.

Spring-loaded umbrellas are handy for carrying in a small bag. When it rains, you take off the cover, release the catch and the umbrella springs open. A squashed spring inside the handle does all the work for you.

Springy hats!

In the 19th century some men wore spring-loaded top hats. At the theatre, they squashed their tall hats under the seats. When the play was over, they let the hats spring back into shape.

13

Spring balances

A spring balance is a simple weighing machine that uses a spring. **Anglers** often use spring balances to weigh their fish.

The weight of the fish stretches the spring. The stretched spring turns a needle around a **dial**. The heavier the fish, the more the spring stretches and the further the needle turns.

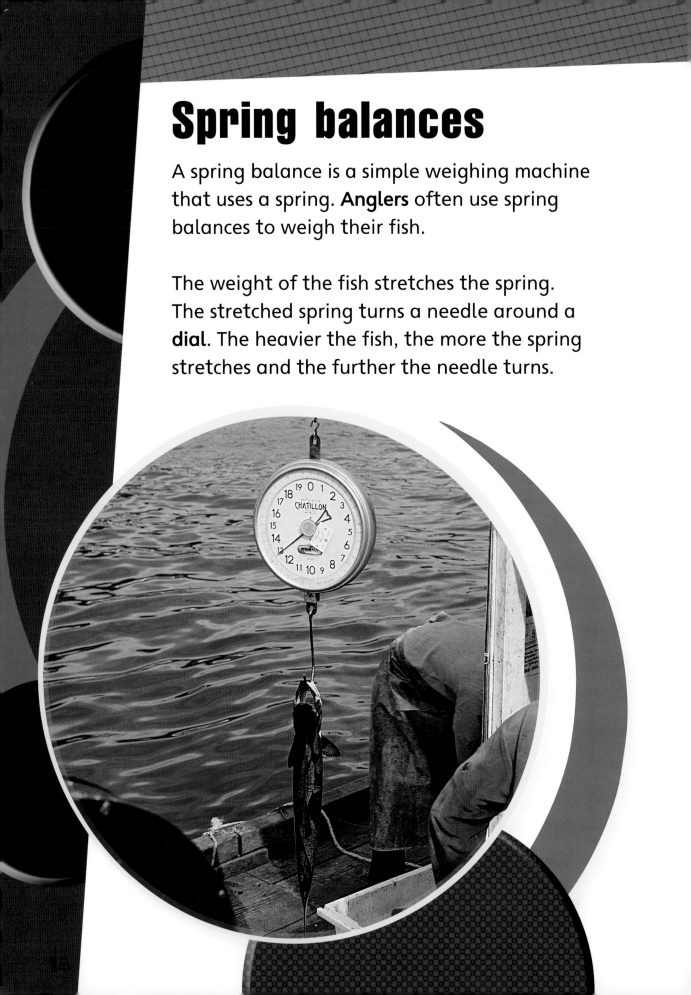

Some bathroom scales have a stiff spring inside. When you stand on the scales the spring inside stretches a small amount. This small movement is **magnified** by **levers**. The levers turn a dial to show your weight.

FACT FILE Stretchy springs

The spring on a spring balance gets longer when you add more weight. A two kilogram fish stretches the spring twice as much as a one kilogram fish.

Spring wheels

Some mountain bikes have springs in their **forks**. The springs squash and stretch when the wheels go over bumps and holes. This makes the ride more comfortable and lets you go faster.

Moto-cross bikes speed round a very rough course. They leap high in the air over the hills and hit the ground again with a jolt. Their long springs help to soften the landing for the rider.

FACT FILE **Leaf springs**

Special sets of springs were invented for horse-drawn carts. They helped to make the passengers comfortable. The springs were made from thin strips of metal stacked together like the leaves of a book.

Clockwork springs

You have to wind up some old clocks with a key. The key winds up a **spiral** spring inside the clock. As the wound-up spring slowly unwinds, it turns the clock hands.

spiral spring

key

The inside of a clock.

Clockwork toys use clock springs to make them move. The clock spring turns a **motor**. In the past, many wonderful toys were powered by clockwork motors. Now most moving toys have electric motors that are powered by **batteries**.

FACT FILE
A wind-up radio!

In 1994, Trevor Baylis invented a clockwork radio that does not need batteries. A clockwork motor turns a tiny machine called a dynamo. The dynamo makes electricity. You can wind up the radio when you want to listen.

Pinballs and cannonballs

A spring fires the steel balls in a pinball machine. When you pull back the plunger it squashes the spring. When you let go, the plunger springs forward and pushes the ball up the table.

Human cannon balls are popular acts at the circus. Although it looks as if the clown is fired from a gun by **gunpowder**, this is only the flash of a firework. It is really a big spring inside the cannon that pushes the clown up into the air.

FACT FILE Stapling springs

A staple gun has a strong spring inside. When you squeeze the handle you squash the spring. Then a catch releases the spring and the gun fires a staple to stick your poster to the wall.

Activities

Making a spring

1. You need a piece of thin fuse wire about 20 cm long.
2. Wind the wire around a pencil in a spiral.

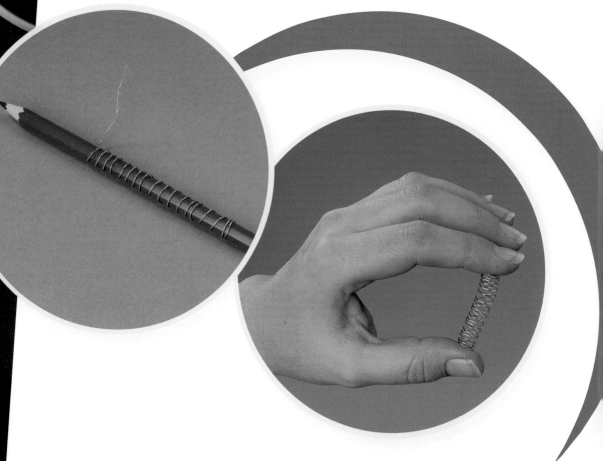

3. Remove the pencil. Now you have a spring.
4. Squeeze the top and bottom of the spring gently and let go. What happens?

See page 4 to find out more about this.

Measuring weight

1. Measure the length of the spring you have just made.
2. Tie a thread around the middle of a piece of wood.
3. Tie a loop at the other end of the thread.

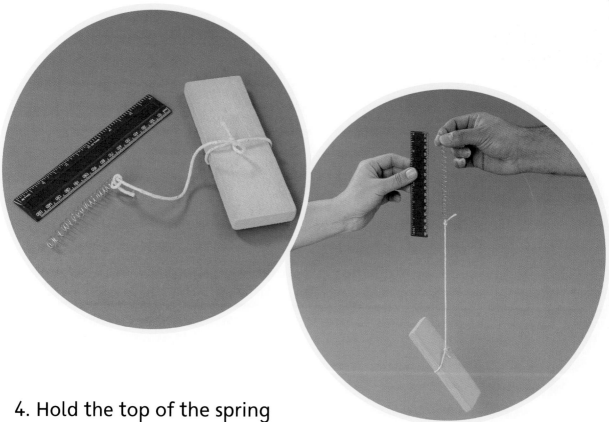

4. Hold the top of the spring and hook the thread to the other end.
5. Measure the length of the spring now that the piece of wood is hanging from it.

Glossary

angler someone who uses a rod and line to catch fish

batteries small packages of chemicals that make electricity

catch the piece of metal that clicks into a slot to keep a door closed

compressed when something is squeezed or squashed

dial the part of a weighing machine where a pointer moves along a row of numbers to show you the weight

dynamo a machine which makes electricity

forks the pair of rods or arms that hold the front wheel of a bicycle

gunpowder powdered chemicals that burn with a flash and a bang

lever a rod or a bar which turns around a hinge or pivot

magnify to make bigger

moto-cross bike motor cycle for racing over rough ground

motor machine that uses electricity or fuels such as petrol or coal to make things move

spiral special shape that goes along and around at the same time. A corkscrew is a spiral shape.

spring loaded held in place by a spring

tension when something is being pulled or stretched

work the energy you use to move something or wind something up

Index